How to Cat Food

Learn How to Feed Your Cat With Delicious, Homemade Recipes so It Can Be Happy and Healthy

By Manuel Hollis

© **Copyright 2021 - All rights reserved.**

The content contained within this book may not be reproduced, duplicated or transmitted without direct written permission from the author or the publisher.

Under no circumstances will any blame or legal responsibility be held against the publisher or author for any damages, reparation, or monetary loss due to the information contained within this book. Either directly or indirectly.

Legal Notice:

This book is copyright protected. This book is only for personal use. You cannot amend, distribute, sell, use, quote or paraphrase any part, or the content within this book, without the consent of the author or publisher.

Disclaimer Notice:

Please note the information contained within this document is for educational and entertainment purposes only. All effort has been executed to present accurate, up to date and reliable, complete information. No warranties of any kind are declared or implied. Readers acknowledge that the author is not engaging in the rendering of legal, financial, medical or professional advice. The content within this book has been derived from various sources. Please consult a licensed professional before attempting any techniques outlined in this book.

By reading this document, the reader agrees that under no

circumstances is the author responsible for any losses, direct or indirect, which are incurred as a result of the use of information contained within this document, including, but not limited to, —errors, omissions, or inaccuracies.

Contents

Food Recipes 1
   Cat Cookies 1
   Crispy Trout Supper 2
   Healthy Powder 3
   Cat Breakfast 4
   Cat Taco 4
   Cat Snacks 5
   Meaty Oats 6
   Precious Cat Treats 8
   Sardine Soup 9
   Sardine Paradise 10
   Salmon Smashers 11
   Happy Cat Meal 12
   Catnip Tea 13
   Cat Biscuits 13
   Cat Paradise 15
   Cat Rolls 16
   Recipe for Picky Eaters 17
   Fishballs 17
   Chicken Soup 18
   Chicken and Sardines 19
   Cheese Please 20
   Birthday Meal 20
   Veggie and Beef Broth 21

Mackerel Munchies 22

Mini-Cat Cakes 22

Baby Kittycat Formula 23

Cat Pudding 24

Cat Hash 26

Chicken Crunchies 26

Chicken and Pasta Stew 27

Crackers 28

Eating Plan for Weight Loss 29

Emergency Kitty Milk 29

Chicken Cheeseburger 30

Catnip Cookies 31

Mackerel Magic 33

Potatoes Au Feline 33

Tuna Patties 34

Tuna Balls 35

Cat Yum Yums 36

Cat Wrap 37

Christmas Reward 38

Cat Munchie 38

Chicken Stir Fry 39

Tuna Treats 39

Sauteed Liver 41

Meowsli 41

Cat Cookies 42

Actually Tasty Salad 43

Salmon Snacks	44
Grain-Free Cat Food	45
Cat Eggs	45
Tutti Frutti	46
A Lil' Ball of Love	46
Husky Goodness	47
Salmon Mouse Mousse	48
Fancy Soup	49
Fishy Pleasure	50
Cat Frenzy	51
Mince Surprise	52
Honey Casserole	53
Salmon Pate	53
Sardine Surprise Treats	54
Cat Kisses	55
Kitty Milk	55
Kipper Supreme	57
Ham Cat Treats	58
Canadian Relish	59
Kitty Snack	59
Meat Majesty	60
Bland Option for Picky Cats	61
CAT'S KIBBLES	61
Mouseburger Bites	63
A+ Supper	63
Yummy Cat Food	64

Liver Cookies 66

Kedgeree 66

Homemade Meal 67

Feline Feast 68

You Got to Have Sole 70

Remedies and Supplies 72

Eating Plan for Kidney Issues 72

Diarrhea Solution 73

Special Supper (Helpful for Cats With Kidney Issues or Diabetes) 74

Pregnant Eating Plan 75

Baking Soda Dry Shampoo 76

Sleeping Pillows for Repelling Fleas 77

Flea Proofing 77

Hairball Treatment 78

Litter Box Deodorizer 78

Litter Box Cleaner and Disinfectant 78

Thank you for buying this book and I hope that you will find it useful. If you will want to share your thoughts on this book, you can do so by leaving a review on the Amazon page, it helps me out a lot.

Food Recipes

Cat Cookies

1 cup entire wheat flour

1/3 cup of milk

1 tsp catnip

1/3 cup of powdered milk

2 tbl vegetable oil or butter

1 egg

1/4 cup of Soy flour

1 tbl Unsulfured molasses

2 tbl Wheat germ

Pre-heat oven to 360 degrees. Blend dry components together. Include molasses, oil, egg, and milk. Roll out straight on an oiled cookie sheet and chop into little, bite-sized bits. Bake for 20-25 minutes and allow it to cool. Stock the cookies in a closed container.

Crispy Trout Supper

1 egg yolk

1 tbl vegetable oil

3 tbl oatmeal

1 little trout fillet

Pre-heat the oven to 350 degrees. Beat the egg, soak the fish within it, and after that, layer with oatmeal. Place the oil in a little baking pan and set the fillet within it, turning it over one or two times. Bake for 20 minutes, flip over and bake for 15 additional minutes. Take out the fish, enable it to cool. Slice into bite-sized bits.

Recommendation: if it appears a bit dry, include a touch of cream.

Healthy Powder

2 cups of nutritional yeast

1/4 cup of kelp powder

1 cup lecithin granules

1/4 cup bonemeal

1,000 mg vitamin C (ground)

Combine all components together in a 1-quart jar and place in the fridge. Include in every recipe. You might likewise include this mix to commercial foods like this: 1 to 2 teaspoons daily for kitties.

Cat Breakfast

3 eggs

3 tbl grated cheese.

2 tbl milk.

1 tbl margarine.

Beat yolks and eggs together. Mix in the grated cheese. Thaw the margarine in a pan up until it sizzles. Include the egg mix, whisking continually up until done.

Cat Taco

1/2 pound ground beef.

1 teaspoon corn oil.

1 tbsp tomato paste.

1/2 teaspoon bone meal.

1 corn tortilla, chopped into kitty-bite-size bits.

1/2 teaspoon brewers' yeast.

2 tablespoons cheddar cheese, grated.

1/2 teaspoon iodized salt.

Heat skillet and begin to sautee ground beef. When meat is half prepared, include bell pepper. Cook the combination up until onions are clear, and the meat golden brown. On lower heat, whisk tomato paste, sliced tortilla, corn oil, brewers' yeast, bone meal, and salt. Whisk up until warmed.

Chill and offer with grated cheese. Yields 2-3 portions. Keep unused parts in a closed container and keep in the fridge. This might be given to your cat one or two times per week.

Cat Snacks

1-1/2 cups rolled oats

1/2 cup tuna oil, beef bouillon or chicken broth

1/2 cup flour

1/4 cup vegetable oil

Pre-heat oven to 360 degrees F. Blend all components into a dough. Cover hands with flour and create little, 1/2-inch dense, round biscuits. Put on greased cookie sheet. Bake for thirty minutes or up until biscuits are a little browned. Cool for thirty minutes prior to offering.

Meaty Oats

4 cups of rolled oats prepared up until soft

2 pounds of minced lean beef, or various other meats. e.g. chicken, rabbit, turkey, or lamb

2 eggs

1 tablespoon of 'Supplement' powder (see beneath).

2 tablespoons of bonemeal or 2 teaspoons of eggshell powder. or 4,000 mg Calcium

2 tablespoons of vegetable oil.

1 teaspoon of fresh raw veggies, e.g. carrot, herbs, spinach, and so on

150 i.u of Vitamin E.

10,000 i.u of Vitamin A from, for instance, cod liver oil.

First include 4 cups of cooked rolled oats, and after that, include the remaining ingredients raw. This is going to make approximately 12 cups of which you feed 1 to 2 cups per day depending upon how big and active your cat is. A bit of liver could be included in the dish, however, do not utilize simply liver as the sole meat.

SUPPLEMENT POWDER:

2 cups of brewers yeast or nutritional yeast.

1/4 cup of Kelp powder.

1000 mg of Vitamin C

1 cup of Lecithin powder.

Blend together and place in the fridge and utilize in the dish above.

Precious Cat Treats

1 12-oz can of salmon with fluid

1/2 cup flour

1/2 cup instant oatmeal, ground

1 egg

Mix the egg and salmon in a mixer; blend up until smooth. Include the oatmeal and mix properly. Apply cooking spray on a 9-by-13inch pan and spread out the mix in the pan. Bake at 360 degrees for half an hour. Chill, then chop into bite-sized squares. Put in the freezer. Produces approximately 24 treats.

Sardine Soup

2 canned sardines

1 cup of water

a couple of watercress stalks

pat of butter

fish sauce (optional).

Place the sardines and the pat of butter within a heavy-based frying-pan and put on medium heat. As the pan warms up and the butter liquefies, mash the sardines within it. When the butter has actually entirely melted, put in the water and whisk as it comes to a boil. Completely shred the watercress and throw it into the pan. Take the pan from the heat and enable it to cool. Puree, and include a bit of fish sauce.

Sardine Paradise

Components:

2 Flat sardine cans in oil (don't drain).

1 Pureed liver

1/4 C Sliced parsley.

2/3 C Cooked rice.

Instructions:

Mix all components and blend properly. Forming into balls of the wanted size or just spoon into cat's meal and offer. These treats might be kept in the fridge for approximately 3 days, and might likewise be frozen.

Salmon Smashers.

Components:

1/2 Prepared smoked salmon (in case your cat is hungry/big, you may do more).

Ham

Regular or cat milk.

chopped cheese (cooked).

Instructions:

Put a bit of the milk into a saucer. Put the salmon within the milk and allow every side to soak for 15 minutes. Wrap the cheese and ham round the salmon and offer it to your kitty!

Happy Cat Meal

Components:

1/2 C Milk

3 pieces of meat, 4 crab sticks or 2 veggies.

1/2 C Flour

1 Egg

Instructions:

Mix all components and utilize a cookie cutter to chop into little shapes. Prepare at 360 F, up until golden brown

Catnip Tea

Components:

1 C Water

2 T Catnip

Instructions:

Place the catnip in a bottle, put the water in. Place the cap on the bottle, and shake up until the catnip tea becomes green.

Cat Biscuits

1 pound liver, organs, or other meat

2 cups of bran

1/4 cup of cooking oil

2 cups of old-fashioned oatmeal

Preheat oven to 260 degrees F. Use cool water to cover the meat and bring to a boil. Instantly reduce heat and simmer for thirty minutes. Take out the meat from water and allow it to cool; keep the water for now.

When the meat is totally cool, slice into 1-inch bits and slice in a mixer or grind in a food processor, or refine via a meat grinder up until it is carefully ground. Blend ground meat, oatmeal, bran, and oil, including the cooking water from the meat as needed to make a thick dough. Stay clear of utilizing any more liquid than required to create a dough that is coarse and adequately damp to deal with. Form the dough into small bone shapes or flattened balls and place on an oiled baking sheet. Bake for 3 hours. Then, shut off the heat and allow the biscuits to cool in the oven to guarantee they are crispy and tough. Allow the biscuits to air dry for a day and keep in a sealed container on the shelf for as much as 4 weeks.

KEEP IN MIND: When creating this dish, form the biscuits into little bits for easier chewing.

TIP: A great suggestion for getting the meat for this dish is to put organs from turkeys, chickens, and so on in a plastic bag in the freezer up until you have what you need to create this tasty delight.

Cat Paradise

2 cups of sardines in oil.

1 tbl liver.

2/3 cup prepared rice.

1/4 cup parsley, sliced.

Mix all components. Whisk with a wood spoon to split sardines into bite-sized pieces. Keep unused pieces in a fridge, securely covered.

Cat Rolls

1 flour tortilla.

1 cup ground chicken.

1/8 cup chicken broth.

1/8 cup of low-fat cream

1 teaspoon salt.

Blending bowl.

Blend chicken broth with ground chicken within the blending bowl. After these are blended, put the chicken on the center of the tortilla. Include 1/8 cup of cream and 1 teaspoon of salt atop the chicken. Now roll up just 2 sides of the tortilla up until they get to one another. Tuck the other sides atop the rolled-up sides up until they meet. Offer to your kitty!

Recipe for Picky Eaters

1 cup chicken, microwaved or boiled

1/4 cup steamed, shredded carrots.

1/4 cup steamed, fresh broccoli.

Chicken broth.

Mix components with adequate chicken broth to hold together. This identical dish could be utilized with fish (microwave or broil up until it flakes.) You can likewise vary the dish by including rice or other veggies.

Fishballs

3 baby carrots, prepared up until soft.

2 oz prepared herring, skin extracted.

16 oz canned tuna in olive oil, drained.

2-3 tbl grated cheese.

2 tbl oatmeal or whole grain bread crumbs.

2 tsp brewer's yeast.

1 egg, beaten.

2 tbl tomato paste

Numerous pinches of sliced catnip.

Pre-heat the oven to 360 *. Grind the carrots with the bread crumbs, fish or oatmeal, brewer's yeast, cheese, egg, catnip, and tomato paste to a uniform paste. Form into little balls and place on an oiled baking tray. Bake for 15-20 minutes, inspecting regularly: the fish balls ought to be golden brown and solid. Cool completely.

Chicken Soup

Mix 1 chicken liver, 1 chicken heart, 1 giblet, 1 chicken neck, 1 tablespoon carefully sliced parsley and 2 cups of water.

Cover and simmer up until the giblet is soft. For kitties, grind the meat in the mixer.

Chicken and Sardines

1 can of sardines in olive oil

1 egg, beaten

1/4 cup whole-grain bread crumbs

2 prepared chicken drumsticks, bones extracted

1/2 tsp brewer's yeast

Drain the sardines, keeping the olive oil, and grind. Blend in the bread crumbs, yeast and an egg to an uniform, viscous consistency. Cover the chicken drumsticks uniformly in the mix. Heat the reserved olive oil in a pan, then include the layered drumsticks and fry, flipping often, up until brown. Extract from the heat, and cool prior to offering.

Cheese Please

1/2 cup grated cheese

A bit of oatmeal

2 tbs low-fat spread or margarine

2 tbs sour cream or plain yogurt

Grind all of the components together, including them in the order showed above, and offer cold. No cooking is needed for this meal. Some felines are going to not take to this meal as it is not meaty. other cats are going to adore it.

Birthday Meal

1 - 2 poached fish, ideally salmon, with the bones and skin extracted

A couple of drops of fresh lemon juice

1 tsp. plain yogurt

Poach the fish. Then blend the lemon juice yogurt and offer over the prepared fish.

Veggie and Beef Broth

1/2 cup of raw cut beef

2 tablespoons prepared oatmeal.

1 tablespoon dried barley grass powder

A couple of tablespoons of beef broth

1 cooked minced vegetable (Carrots are frequently preferred).

Prepare raw cut beef in sufficient amount of broth to cover, across low to medium heat. When beef is prepared, scrap with a fork and blend with the broth in which it was cooked. Include the minced vegetable and the barley grass powder. Whisk properly. Last, include the oatmeal to get the consistency that your feline likes. This is an excellent feline food dish for indoor animals.

Mackerel Munchies

1/2 cup canned mackerel, drained.

1 tablespoon veggie oil.

1 cup whole-grain bread crumbs.

1/2 teaspoon brewer's yeast, optional.

1 egg, beaten.

Preheat oven to 360 degrees F. Within a medium-size bowl, grind the mackerel with a fork into small pieces. Mix it with the lingering components and blend properly. Drop it all by 1/4 teaspoonsful onto an oiled cookie sheet. Bake for 7 minutes. Cool to area temperature level and keep in a closed container in the fridge.

Mini-Cat Cakes

2 cups entire wheat flour

1 cup water or skimmed milk

1 tablespoon honey

1/2 cup soybean flour

1 teaspoon sea salt

1 tablespoon Canola or Sunflower oil

Blend dry components. Include honey and liquid. Blend and allow the dough to rest in a warm location for 15 minutes. Include oil and permit to sit another 30 minutes. Take walnut-size parts of dough and squash into little cakes. Bake in an oven at 390 degrees for 30 minutes.

Baby Kittycat Formula

1 can of milk (evaporated)

1 entire egg.

1 cup Pedialyte (or common equivalent, un-processed).

1/2 teaspoon liquid infant vitamins.

1 package un-processed gelatin.

Mixed together. Heat tiny amounts in the microwave to "comfy" temperature level instantly prior to administering. Keep leftovers in the fridge for no more than 72 hours. Mix prior to offering every time.

To administer, utilize a kitty feeding bottle or a syringe without a needle. Begin with little amounts and work up slowly as the kitty grows. Administer one time every 2 hours throughout the initial 2 weeks, every 3 hours throughout the 3rd week, every 4 hours throughout the 4th week. Throughout the 4th week, begin mixing a little can of top quality ground cat food into the combination.

Cat Pudding

This pudding is abundant in calcium and could be supplied as a supplement for lactating queens, weaning kitties, or ill cats.

250ml evaporated milk

250ml boiling water.

2 tablespoons of high-calorie mayo.

2 egg yolks (dispose of the whites).

2 tablespoons of corn syrup.

2 tablespoons of plain yogurt.

Cat vitamins.

1 pill acidophilus (or utilize acidophilus yogurt).

Liquify gelatin in 250ml boiling water and leave to cool. Include all components that remain to cooled gelatin. Put the combination in the fridge. The mix is going to gel as it chills and could be scraped out as needed. Warm the combination a little in the microwave prior to serving.

Do not return the heated mix to the primary supply. The mix could be kept in the fridge for 7 days or frozen up until required.

at Hash

1/2 cup prepared brown rice

1 cup prepared ground beef

3/4 cup of creamy cottage cheese

6 tbl. alfalfa sprouts

Blend together and offer.

Chicken Crunchies

1-1/2 cups of rye flour.

1-1/2 cups of whole-wheat flour.

1 cup wheat germ.

1-1/2 cups of brown rice flour.

1 teaspoon garlic powder.

1 teaspoon alfalfa or dried kelp.

4 tablespoons vegetable oil.

1 pound ground chicken.

1 to 2 tablespoons brewer's yeast.

1 1/2 cups of beef broth or chicken broth.

Pre-heat the oven to 360 degrees F. In a big bowl, mix the initial 6 dry components. Gradually include oil, chicken and broth, and blend properly. On a gently floured exterior, roll the dough to a density of 1/8 inch, and after that, put it on a oiled cookie sheet. Bake up until golden brown.

Cool, and after that, crack into bite-size bits. Put bits in a bag with the brewer's yeast and shake to layer them. Keep the leftovers in a closed container in the fridge. Creates 20 to 30 pieces.

Chicken and Pasta Stew

2 packages ground turkey or chicken.

2-3 cups macaroni (Prepared).

2-3 little carrots, prepared.

Garlic.

2 tablespoons vegetable oil.

Boil the macaroni up until tender. Prepare the chicken in a pan. Blend all the things together in a food processor. Include the garlic and the oil. Blend properly.

Crackers

6 ounces of undrained tuna.

1 cup flour.

1/3 cup water.

1 cup cornmeal.

Pre-heat the oven to 360 degrees. Place all of the components into a bowl and blend completely with your hands. Roll out to 0.25 inch density and chop into snack-sized bits. Put on an oiled cookie sheet. Bake for approximately 20 minutes or up until golden. Allow it to cool. Offer to your cat.

Eating Plan for Weight Loss

1 pound of chunky or minced lean meat: chicken, turkey heart, and so on, with a bit of liver occasionally.

1/2 cup wheat bran or oats or veggies like beans, peas, corn and carrots.

1-1/2 cups 10 oz. of prepared potatoes or 1 cup of prepared rice.

1, 800 mg of calcium, 1 teaspoon of eggshell powder cat vitamins or 1 tablespoon of bonemeal.

1 teaspoon of grease

Emergency Kitty Milk

1 envelope Knox un-processed gelatin

12 oz. of boiling water

Liquify the gelatin within the boiling water, and include:

2 tablespoons of mayo

1-12 oz. can of evaporated, canned milk

1 tablespoons of light corn syrup

1 egg yolk

2 tablespoons of plain yogurt

Blend effectively in a mixer. Put in a covered bowl and keep it in a fridge. Heat a tiny amount for feedings. This is going to keep for approximately 7 days.

Chicken Cheeseburger

2 oz carefully ground chicken

2 oz carefully ground beef

1 tbs canned dense chicken soup

2 oz oatmeal or whole-grain bread crumbs

1 baby carrot, prepared up until soft

1/2 cup grated cheese

1 egg

Mash the chicken and meat with the soup, and after that, include the oatmeal or bread crumbs, mushy carrot and egg. Form into 2 little hamburgers and broil. Add grated cheese and broil once again up until the cheese is liquefied. Enable to cool up until warm to the touch, and offer.

Catnip Cookies

2 tablespoons wheat germ

1 cup whole-wheat flour

1/3 cup of confectioners' milk

1/4 cup of soy flour

1/2 teaspoon of bonemeal

1 tablespoon of kelp

1 tablespoon of unsulfured molasses

1 teaspoon crushed dried catnip leaves

1/3 cup water or milk

2 tablespoons oil, fat or butter

1 egg

Blend the dry components together. Include the molasses, oil, egg, fat or butter and water or milk. Turn out flat on a greased cookie sheet and chop into slim ribbons or strips. Bake at 360 ° F for 15 minutes or up until gently toasted.

Split into pea-size bits, appropriate for felines. Great for delights, cleaning teeth and working out gums, however, too low in protein to utilize for a routine fare.

Mackerel Magic

1 fresh mackerel, headed, cleaned, scaled, and tailed.

2 tsp soy sauce, fish or Worcestershire sauce

2 pieces of unsmoked bacon, broiled

1 cup prepared brown rice

Slice the bacon up little and blend with the rice, including the sauce in touches as you go. Broil the mackerel on each side up until crispy brown. Enable to cool, then divide it along the stomach and carefully open it out. Bone, going from the tail to head. Load with the bacon mix and rice, close over the mackerel sides and offer.

Potatoes Au Feline

2 tbl grated veggies

3 cups boiled chopped potatoes

1 tbl Nutritional yeast

1/2 cup creamed cottage cheese

1/4 cup whole milk

2 tbl grated carrots

1/4 cup grated cheese

Coat the initial 5 components into a casserole meal. Then put the milk atop all; spray with cheese. Bake approximately 15 minutes at 360F up until cheese liquefies and browns somewhat. Offer cool.

As a potato alternative, you may utilize 3 cups prepared brown rice or 3 cups of prepared oatmeal.

Tuna Patties

1/4 cup pureed liver

1/2 cup boiled rice

2-3 sprigs sliced parsley

Drain the tuna and blend all the things together. Create 6-7 balls, and after that, pat them into patties. Keep in the refrigerator and offer to your feline. This is one feline delight dish that your feline buddy will not be picky about.

Tuna Balls

Components:

1/2 C Cut chicken or turkey.

2/3 c Dry Feline Food

1 Can Drained tuna

Chopped veggies (optional).

Instructions:

Mix all components in a little bowl up until well combined. Make into little balls or anything you are comfy with. Cool for approximately an hour. Afterwards, cover the balls in bread crumbs or something crunchy.

Cat Yum Yums

Components:

1/4 C Warm milk or water.

3 T Catni

1/2 C Dry cat food.

Instructions:

Place the milk and cat food in the bowl and blend properly. Empty any additional water. Spray the catnip over the combination and blend well. In case you want, you might bake in a 360-degree oven for 15 minutes.

Cat Wrap

Components:

1/8 C Chicken Broth.

1/8 C Cream (Low Fat).

1 Flour Tortilla.

1 t Salt.

1 C Ground Chicken.

Instructions:

Blend the chicken broth with ground chicken. After blended, put the chicken on the center of the tortilla. Include cream and salt atop the chicken, and after that, roll up the tortilla.

Christmas Reward

1/2 mashed prepared pumpkin.

1 cup minced remaining turkey.

1 tablespoon kelp.

1 tablespoon oil.

Blend together and form into balls. Give as a snack or provide as x-mas gifts to your cat!

Cat Munchie

1 tablespoon milk.

2 eggs.

2 tablespoons carefully sliced alfalfa sprouts.

3 tablespoons cottage cheese.

Blend all components together. Put into a hot pan with a tablespoon of butter or vegetable oil. When brown down, flip over and brown the opposite side. Slice into bits and offer.

Chicken Stir Fry

Chop raw chicken breast. Warm oil in fry pan or a wok, and prepare the meat rapidly on top of a high flame, whisking constantly. When the chicken is nearly prepared, whisk in a couple of flaked almonds for included crunch. Enable to cool and offer with a bit of plain boiled rice.

Tuna Treats

1/2 cup nonfat, powdered, dry milk.

1/2 cup whole wheat flour.

1/2 can tuna, in oil OR 1/2 cup cooked chicken, sliced into little pieces.

1 Tablespoon cod liver oil OR veggie oil

1/4 cup water.

1 egg, beaten.

Catnip (Optional).

Preheat oven to 360 degrees and oil cookie sheets by using cooking spray. In a big bowl, grind the chicken or tuna into tinier bits. Then include milk and flour. Blend properly. When all is blended, put in oil and water. Blend properly once again. Now, beat the egg in a different recipe up until the egg gets a foamy texture. Include in the mix. Blend properly. The dough mix is going to be sticky, so do not fret. Utilizing your fingers form dough into little bite-size balls, approximately the size of a marble. Place balls on oiled cookie sheets. Squash and bake for 10 minutes. Take out snack from oven, wait 5 minutes and flip treats over, so the opposite side is going to cook. Bake for 12 more minutes or up until golden brown. Put snack on a cookie rack to chill for 10 minutes.

Sauteed Liver

Heat 1 teaspoon corn oil in a pan. Include 1/4 pound beef liver and fry on each side up until prepared yet not dry within. Include 1/2 cup water to the pan and blend it with all the brown pieces. Grind the liver within a mixer, utilizing the pan juices.

Meowsli

1/2 banana, mashed

1 tablespoon oats

1/2 cup orange juice

2 tablespoon plain yogurt

2 ounces berries in season

1/4 apple, sliced

Blend bananas and oats, mixing properly. Include yogurt, apple, and orange juice instantly to stop browning. Mash berries and include them in the mix. Offer in tiny portions (1 tablespoon per cat); excessive fruit can trigger diarrhea in a gastrointestinal system which is not accustomed to it.

Cat Cookies

1 cup whole wheat flour

1 teaspoon catnip

1 egg

1/4 cup soy flour

2 tablespoons wheat germ

1/3 cup milk

1/3 cup powdered milk

2 tablespoons vegetable oil or butter

1 tablespoon unsulfured molasses

Preheat oven to 360 degrees. Blend dry components. Include molasses, oil, egg, and milk. Turn out flat onto a greased cookie sheet and chop into little, bite-sized bits. Bake for 15 minutes. Allow it to cool and keep in a firmly sealed container.

Actually Tasty Salad

1 little carrot grated and peeled.

1/2 cup sliced alfalfa sprouts

1/4 cup grated and peeled zucchini

1/8 cup chicken stock

1/4 tsp fresh or dried catnip

1 tsp. carefully sliced parsley

Mix veggies in a medium bowl. Include chicken stock and shake. Spray with catnip and offer at room temperature level. Keep leftovers in the fridge for approximately 3 days.

Salmon Snacks

Components:

Salmon (prepared).

Dry cat food

Cat Snack

Instructions:

1. Cut a small piece of cooked salmon. Make certain it is still wet, though.

2. Afterward, take your cat's preferred snack and press it into the wet salmon.

3. Take a bit of dry feline food and squash a smidgen up. Spray the squashed food on the Salmon.

Grain-Free Cat Food

1 pound ground turkey, beef or chicken.

1/3 cup broccoli diced in a mixer.

1/3 cup grated carrots.

4-8 vitamins tablets powdered.

1/4 cup liver pureed in a mixer.

Mix everything together. Place in ice trays and freeze. Get them out and melt as required.

Cat Eggs

dry cat food.

1 or 2 eggs.

Sausage.

Chop up the sausage into little bites, and then take the eggs, and place in a pot, and include the sausage and cat food and serve.

Tutti Frutti

1 teaspoon minced cantaloupe.

1 teaspoon minced seedless grapes.

2 teaspoons cottage cheese.

1 teaspoon minced watermelon.

In a bowl, mix the cottage cheese and fruit. Offer as a snack.

A Lil' Ball of Love

3 tablespoons of cat milk.

1 can of moist cat food.

A handful of dry food.

Blend the milk and canned cat food up until slushy. Then include a bit of dry food and stir. For an included benefit of your cat, you can include a bit of tuna too.

Husky Goodness

1/2 cup raw trimmed beef

2 tablespoons prepared oatmeal

1 tablespoon beef broth

1 prepared minced vegetable

1 tablespoon dried barley grass powder

Cook raw cut beef in sufficient amount of broth to cover, accross low to medium heat. When beef is prepared, cut with a fork and combine with the broth where it was prepared. Include the minced vegetable (carrots are excellent here) and the barley grass powder. Whisk properly. Finally, include the oatmeal to attain the consistency that your feline enjoys.

Salmon Mouse Mousse

1/2 cup skimmed milk.

4 oz prepared salmon, bones and skin extracted.

1 drop of red food coloring.

1 tbl softened margarine or creamed, low fat spread.

Approximately 1/2 cup prepped gelatin.

A couple of cooked, shelled shrimps.

Squish the prepared salmon and slowly include the milk; additionally, place the milk and the cooked salmon in a food processor or blender and refine up until velvety. Whisk in the low-fat spread or margarine, include the food coloring, and beat intensely up until stiff. Place in a molf or a glass bowl to ensure that the mix fills it by three-quarters. Cool for 20 minutes, and then embellish with the prepared shrimp, and pour on simply sufficient heated gelatin to cover them. When this layer has actually set, include additional gelatin for taste and leave for around 60 minutes in a cool location or the refrigerator.

To offer, flip the mousse onto a plate and sp into servings.

Fancy Soup

1 hard-boiled egg

7 big pinches of garlic

1 can tuna

1 raw egg

1 capful of olive oil

Rice

1 cup of water

Do not utilize this dish daily, however, it's excellent for those unique events. Pour in the hard-boiled egg, water, olive oil, garlic, and as much rice as you desire. Then squeeze the liquid out of the can of tuna and blend them entirely. Slice up the hard-boiled egg, place all the things into the pan, and when boiling, put in the raw egg. Boil for 10 minutes and offer.

Fishy Pleasure

2 eggs.

2 tablespoons supplemental powder.

1 tablespoon bone meal.

1-2 cups milk.

100-200 IU vitamin E.

2,500 IU vitamin A.

200 mg Taurine.

1 tablespoon veggie oil.

1 tablespoon fresh raw veggies.

4 pieces of brown bread.

1 can of tuna or mackerel.

Mix together milk, eggs and supplements, and after that, blend properly with bread and fish. Offer raw or baked for 20 minutes approximately at 170 C.

Cat Frenzy

Components:

1 Can damp cat food.

1/2 C dry cat food.

2 t Feline milk.

Instructions:

1. Scrape the damp supper into Kitty's food meal and mush it so that it remains in minimal bits with Cat's fork.

2. Crush dry cat food using a potato masher on the ziplock bag. Spray that beaten food on the damp supper.

3. Suck up the initial piece of feline milk using an eyedropper and place it on the damp supper and dry food and follow with the final piece of feline milk.

4. Place into the microwave for a couple of seconds and offer to your cat!

Mince Surprise

Components:

3 T Rice.

100 g meat (minced).

1 T gravy or Broth.

Instructions:

Sizzle the meat for 10 minutes or up until red and good. Include a bit of water if it gets adhered to the pan. Then include the rice in addition to an additional spoon of water if you desire the meal to be slushy. Whisk in the broth or gravy, depending upon cat's taste. Take off the heat, and allow it cool, and after that, offer. The diced chicken might be used instead of minced meat.

Honey Casserole

Components:

1 t Honey.

1 Can Tuna.

Extra garnishes

Cat's preferred food.

Instructions:

Mix together and offer.

Salmon Pate

1/4 cup of bread crumbs.

1 (6 ounce) can of skinless, boneless salmon.

1 beaten egg.

1/2 cup carefully sliced celery.

1/2 cup of water.

1 unflavored gelatin envelope.

Preheat oven to 330 degrees F. Mix all components and blend properly. Load into a little fish-shaped mold and bake for 40 minutes. Offer at regular temperature level.

Sardine Surprise Treats

2 flat cans of sardines in oil (Don't drain).

1/4 cup sliced parsley.

1 tablespoon pureed liver.

2/3 cup prepared rice.

Mix all components and blend well. Form into balls of the wanted size or merely spoon into cat's meal and offer. These treats might be kept in the fridge for approximately 3 days, and might likewise be frozen.

Cat Kisses

Bag or can of kitty food.

Ziploc bag with the cut corned.

Catnip (optional).

Place cat food and possible catnip within A food processor or blender and blend up until it appears like frosting.

Place the mix within the Ziploc bag and squeeze small droppings, or "kisses" on a cookie sheet and bake in 310 degrees F. Time depends upon the size of kisses. Little ones require around 15 minutes.

Kitty Milk

12 ounces evaporated milk

13 ounces unflavored Pedialyte

8 ounces plain yogurt (1% milkfat and NOT light).

2 egg yolks.

2-1/2 ounces of lamb baby food.

2 tablespoons Karo white corn syrup.

Place all components into a mixer and blend properly. Place milk within Nurse-Maid animal nursing bottle and warm to lukewarm. Make certain to whisk the milk in the container every time prior to filling up the bottle. Put milk that remains into 8-ounce containers and freeze up until required. Two-week-old kitties are going to consume approximately 1/2 ounces every 4 hours. Four week-old kitties are going to consume approximately 1 to 1-1/2 ounces every 5 hours.

Kipper Supreme

1 cup remaining cooked root veggies.

4 oz prepared kipper.

A bit of milk.

1/2 cup of grated cheese.

2 eggs.

Pre-heat the oven to 330 degrees. Squish together the veggies and fish. Place the mix into a greased baking pan. Whip the eggs, cheese, and milk together, and put on top of the fish combination. Bake for approximately 20 minutes, up until the exterior is solid and the within is fairly soft. Take out from the oven and let it cool.

Ham Cat Treats

5/8 cup wheat germ.

1 container (2-1/2 ounces) strained ham baby food.

1 egg, beaten.

5/8 cup of non-fat milk powder.

Preheat oven to 360 degrees. Sprinkle cookie sheet with veggie oil spray. Blend baby food, milk powder, wheat germ, and egg in a moderate pot. Put 1/2 teaspoonfuls onto a ready baking sheet. Bake for around 15 minutes. Take out from the oven and allow to cool on a cake rack. Keep baked delight in a plastic bag or closed container and put in freezer or fridge. You can expect 25 to 30 pieces.

KEEP IN MIND: Chicken or beef baby food might be used instead of ham.

Canadian Relish

Simmer 500g white fish and 500g liver carefully in water up until prepared. Soak a cup of dry cat food in half a cup of tomato juice. Drain the fish and liver, extract the bones, however, conserve the fluid. Put all components, plus a single teaspoon of cod liver oil, within a food processor, utilizing the metal blade. Utilize the conserved liquid to change the mix consistency to the kitty's taste.

Kitty Snack

1/2 cup dry cat food

3 tablespoons catnip

1/4 cup milk or warm water

Place the milk and cat food within the pot and blend properly. Empty any additional water. Spray the catnip over the mix and blend properly. In case you want, you might bake in a 360-degree oven for approximately 15 minutes.

Meat Majesty

Components:

1/4 can whitefish + tuna dinner

1/4 can chicken in gravy

1/4 can beef

A bit of dry cat food

1/4 can salmon

Instructions:

Blend together and offer. Place the remainder in the refrigerator to keep fresh.

Bland Option for Picky Cats

1 c Chicken, microwaved or boiled.

Chicken broth

1/4 c Shredded, steamed carrots

1/4 c Fresh, steamed broccoli

Mix components with adequate chicken broth to hold together. This identical dish could be utilized with fish (microwave or broil up until it flakes.) You can likewise change the dish by including rice or various other veggies.

CAT'S KIBBLES

2 cups soy flour

3 cups whole wheat flour

1 cup wheat germ

1 cup non-fat, dry milk

1 cup cornmeal

1 (15 ounce) can mackerel

1/2 cup brewer's yeast

5 tablespoons veggie oil

2 cups of water, or as required

1 tablespoon cod liver oil

Preheat oven to 360 degrees. Blend all the dry components in a big bowl. In an additional bowl, mash the mackerel into little bits. Blend in the water and oil. Include the mackerel mix to the dry components and blend completely. The dough is hard, so utilize your hands. Roll dough out to approximately 1/4" density and chop into 1/4" bits, utilizing a pizza cutter or knife. Pile the pieces onto oiled cookie sheets and bake for 20 minutes. Throughout baking, periodically toss the pieces with 2 wood spoons, so they brown equally. Turn the heat off and enable the delight to cool completely prior to removing and keeping it in a sealed container in the fridge. This dish freezes extremely well for lengthier storage.

Mouseburger Bites

2 tbl oatmeal

3 oz carefully ground beef or sausage meat

hair of catnip, carefully sliced

1 egg, to bind

Knead the components together extremely carefully and shape them into a flat oval. Broil beneath a medium heat for 6 minutes, often turning, up until the exterior is crisp. Wait up until cool, then cut into bite-sized pieces.

A+ Supper

cat food

1/2 of a carrot

1 egg

Milk

Initially boil a half carrot, chop into little pieces when it is soft, and then get a lot of cat food and include 1 egg and milk into a pot of kitty food. (do not place carrots with cat food and milk) Mix till blended, and after that, include carrots.

Yummy Cat Food

Components:

1 cup somewhat cooked or raw organ meat (kidney, heart. liver, lung).

3 cups gently cooked or raw ground meat (chicken, beef, lamb or turkey).

1 cup well-cooked grain (rice, oats, cornmeal or barley).

1 raw turkey neck, carefully sliced or ground (make sure not to cook).

1 raw egg.

1 cup well-cooked veggie (broccoli, carrots, zucchini, green beans or squash).

1 teaspoon flaxseed oil or olive oil.

Instructions:

Mix all components together, and after that, split into particular parts. The less you cook the components, the more nutritious it is going to be for your kitty. If you freeze the particular parts, they are going to keep for a number of weeks and you can thaw one per day. When thawing, attempt not to utilize the microwave or another cooking technique, given that this is going to lower nutrient levels. Rather, let food thaw overnight in the fridge. To warm it, put the food in plastic bags that have a zipper, then submerge the bag in hot water for around 10 minutes.

The quantity of food made with this dish ought to last for approximately 5 days for an adult cat of regular size. Your cat might consume less or more at every meal; utilize sound judgment to choose a serving size. Since this mix is a little lower in calories than dry kitty food, you are going to have to offer a little more of it in contrast.

Liver Cookies

Preheat oven to 360 degrees F. Mix 1/2 cup wheat germ, and 1/2 cup dry milk. Sprinkle 1 teaspoon of honey. Include one 3-1/3 oz. container of homemade mixed liver or strained liver baby food and whisk up until all the things are effectively combined. Shape the combination into balls; put them on a greased cookie sheet and squash them with a fork. Bake 8 to 10 minutes. Consistency ought to be fudgy. Keep in a container in the refrigerator; freeze if keeping more than a couple of days.

Kedgeree

1/3 cup white rice

3 oz smoked mackerel or canned tuna, boned and skinned.

1 tbl margarine or low-fat spread

1/2 tbl pouring cream

1/2 hard-boiled egg, shelled and carefully sliced yolk of 1 egg

Cook and drain the rice. As the rice is cooking, carefully fry the sliced tomato in the margarine up until tender. Include the egg and the fish and keep on cooking, constantly whisking with a wooden spoon. Blend the rice, hold across the heat, and whisk. Mix in the egg yolk, and then the cream. After a final couple of stirs, place onto a plate and enable to cool.

Homemade Meal

2 big hard-cooked eggs.

1/4 pound liver (chicken, beef or pork only).

1/8 teaspoon potassium chloride (salt alternative).

1 tablespoon veggie oil.

1 teaspoon of calcium carbonate.

2 cups prepared white rice with no salt.

Likewise, include a well-balanced supplement which satisfies the cat's daily requirement for all minerals and vitamins and 250mg taurine per day. Dice and braise the meat, keeping the fat. Mix all components and blend properly. This mix is rather dry and the palatability might be enhanced by including a bit of water.

Feline Feast

2 eggs

1 cup of Polenta or cornmeal (Prepare with 4 cups of water and include in the remainder of the components that are fed raw.

2 pounds of minced red or white meat;(liver/kidney/heart/tripe) or fish or a combination.

2 tablespoons of butter or veggie oil (Less in case fatty meats are utilized).

2 tablespoons of bonemeal

4 tables spoons of 'Supplement' Powder (see beneath).

150 i.u. Vitamin E.

10,000 units of Vitamin A (fish oils).

Feed 3/4 to 1-1/2 cups to your kitty with every meal.

1 teaspoon of raw fresh veggies with every meal.

Rice, oats (2 cups prior to cooking), or potatoes (4 cups prepared) could be utilized instead of corn as a grain alternative or a mix. Constantly include approximately 500 mg of Taurine to cat dishes in case you cook the meats.

SUPPLEMENT POWDER:

2 cups of brewers yeast or nutritional yeast.

1000 mg of Vitamin C

1 cup of Lecithin powder.

1/4 cup of Kelp powder.

Blend together; cool and utilize in the dish above.

You Got to Have Sole

2 tbl sliced onion

1/2 pound fillet of sole.

pepper and salt.

2 tbl sliced parsley.

1 tbl butter.

water.

1/2 cup milk.

1 tbl flour.

2 tbl liver.

1/4 cup grated cheddar cheese.

2/3 cup prepared noodles, chopped into kitty-bite-size bits.

1/2 teaspoon iodized salt.

Place sole in a little, oiled baking disk. Spray with parsley, onion, and a touch of pepper and salt. Include sufficient water to simply cover the bottom of the meal. Place in a pre-heated 440 oven for 10 minutes.

Take out from the oven, cool, and chop into kitty-bit-size bits. Melt butter in a little pan. Whisk in flour and heat up until bubbling. Slowly whisk in milk and cook, stirring continuously up until the combination thickens. Include cheese, salt, and liver; and whisk up until cheese has actually melted.

DO NOT BOIL. Include noodles and sliced fish to cheese sauce and whisk. Cool and offer. Makes 4 to 6 portions. Keep unused parts in an airtight canister and keep them in the fridge.

Remedies and Supplies

Eating Plan for Kidney Issues

4 parts carb: Pureed barley flakes and/or baby food creamed corn

1 part veggie: Carefully grated or sliced raw veggie or veggie juice- carrots, alfalfa, and zucchini sprouts are perfect.

2 parts protein: Gently broiled beef or chicken or raw natural egg yolk, utilized with meat, not by itself (you may likewise utilize baby food chicken).

2 teaspoons soft butter.

2 tablespoons Vita-Mineral Mix.

Mix the above components together and stash them in a glass container. Every day blend this into every meal or apply by dropper following the meal:

1/16 teaspoon Pet Tonic (an iron and B vitamin tonic offered by the vet) or 1/2 of a low-potency B complex pill (10 mg level).

1/8 teaspoon blended mineral powder.

1/2 pill or 1/4 teaspoon blended digestive enzymes.

Provide once a week:

400 units of vitamin E (alpha tocopherol).

A pill consisting of 400 units vitamin D and 10,000 units vitamin A.

Diarrhea Solution

1 can consommé.

1/2 cup rice, raw.

2 cups water.

1 big turkey leg.

Boil the entire thing up until the meat falls off the bone. Enable to chill and chop the meat into really little bits. Feed approximately 2 tablespoons per cat a number of times a day.

Special Supper (Helpful for Cats With Kidney Issues or Diabetes)

1 egg.

1 teaspoon shredded carrot (in case you replace other veggies, stay clear of the ones with a great deal of natural sugars).

2 tablespoons baked chicken breast (no skin) minced.

1 tablespoon minced, cooked green beans.

1 tablespoon olive oil (great for protecting against constipation and hair balls - typical to diabetics).

1/3 cup prepared brown rice (unrefined; wild rice is excellent).

Blend all of the components completely with a wooden spoon or in a food processor/blender. It is essential to get the rice blended in very well to ensure that it can't be picked out. (Diabetics require fiber and kitties with kidney failure issues have to restrict their protein consumption, so this serves 2 functions.) Cook in a little Pyrex skillet across low heat, slicing and whisking continuously, up until the egg are at least soft-set.

Cool in air-tight containers, like Rubbermaid, Tupperware, or Zip-Lock baggies. Utilize within 36 hours. Keeps properly in the freezer in Zip-Lock baggies and could be defrosted and heated concurrently in boiling water within the bag.

Pregnant Eating Plan

2 eggs.

1 cup of Polenta or Cornflour cooked with water to provide 4 cups (Oats, couscous or millet could be utilized alternatively).

4 tablespoons of Supplement Powder (see above).

4 cups minced turkey (heart, chicken or lean lamb/beef or bunny).

2 tablespoons of veggie oil.

1-1/2 teaspoons of bonemeal.

100 i.u. vitamin E.

5,000 i.u. of vitamin A.

Raw veggies: 1 teaspoon with every meal.

Baking Soda Dry Shampoo

Baking soda can clean your cat or dog. Simply massage the baking soda on and make sure to rub into the coat. Let a couple of minutes go by and wipe off! The dog smells are going to be gone, and you do not have to get all soaked!

Sleeping Pillows for Repelling Fleas

2 parts rosemary or sage.

1 part chamomile.

1 part catnip.

Herbs might be utilized whole or cut. Blend sufficiently to pack a 2-foot square pillow for a kitty. Stitch the pillowcase out of a hard, washable material like denim.

Flea Proofing

Include in the food for every adult feline:

1/4 level teaspoon garlic powder

1/2 level teaspoon brewer's yeast

Hairball Treatment

Papaya pills

Empty one pill into damp food daily for approximately 3 days.

Litter Box Deodorizer

4 teaspoons dried mint

1 (16 ounce) box baking soda

Include the mint and sodium bicarbonate to cat litter. Whisk it up, and keep it tidy.

Litter Box Cleaner and Disinfectant

1 1/2 cups water

1 tablespoon scented fluid castile soap or fluid hand soap.

1 tablespoon chlorine bleach

Include bleach and soap to a 1-pint plastic spray bottle. Include water and shake. Splash the empty, dry box completely and allow it to sit for 2 minutes. Wash, dry, and replenish with litter.

HANDY TIP: Splash the litter box with non-stick spray to stop the litter from adhering to the litter pan.

I hope that you enjoyed reading through this book and that you have found it useful. If you want to share your thoughts on this book, you can do so by leaving a review on the Amazon page. Have a great rest of the day.

Printed in Great Britain
by Amazon